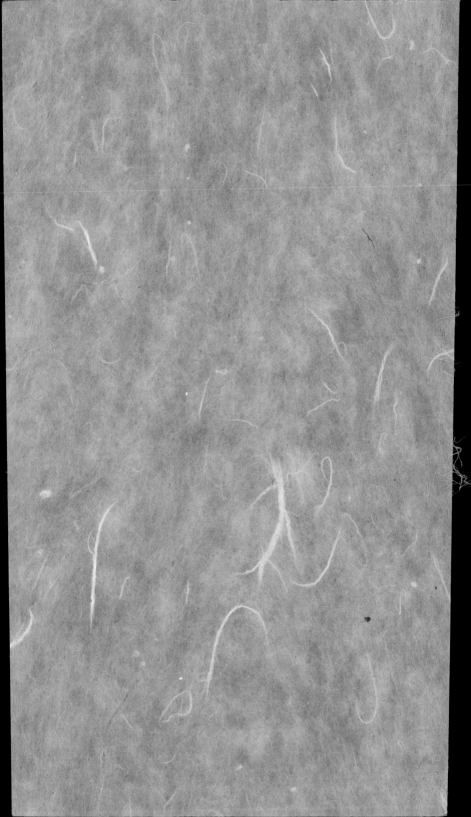

GREEN

Poems by
Marion Boyer

Finishing Line Press
Cincinnati • Georgetown

GREEN

For the men in my life --
Eddie, Jonathan and Andy

This is a limited collector's edition.

ACKNOWLEDGMENTS

These poems have appeared or are forthcoming in the following
journals:

The Atlanta Review: "Elephants Never Forget"
Concho River Review: "Canyon"
Crab Creek Review: "Worm Moon"
The Driftwood Review: "Bioluminescence";
                          "The Constant Hum of the Earth"
Heliotrope: "The Orchard, September 2001"
The MacGuffin: "The Man and the Bluefin Tuna"
Midnight Mind: "The Excavator"
Midwest Quarterly: "The Window";
                       "An Awful Stillness"
The Spoon River Poetry Review: "The Shape of Fear"
Rhino: "Jake, Moonlighting;" "Jake, Dying"

Editor: **Leah Maines**
Cover Art: From an original art work entitled "undercover"
        by **Barbara Andreadis**
Author Photo: **Kenn Livingston**
Printed in the USA.

email: FinishingBooks@aol.com

Author inquiries and orders:

Finishing Line Press
P. O. Box 1016
Cincinnati, Ohio 45201-1016
U. S. A.

Table of Contents

THE WINDOW

In the sudden limbo that follows
a pause of the moon, ivy is the first
to sleep. No. That is not right.
The house wanders; stone, straw,
wind stagger through leaves.
What we owe teaches everything:
the moment to fly in ragged circles, clockwise.
In us, in the bats, there is a kind of weather
painting our stories. I have become
a student of the space inside bone
where song or storm tears a window.
A bell floats there. It is no illusion.
What I mean is, the echoes
are dazzling and they never stop.

RAELIANS

I can't forgive
that they trained
catalpa trees to talk,
reversed the engine
of each hour and cured
rain. Some say
they'll never extend
the back channels
of color, stretch yellow
into a rare new form,
but don't bet on it.
When some infernal
scientist makes a jab
at a petri dish
you can't imagine
what could be behind
his goggle-bloated eyes.

METAMORPHOSIS

There is nothing left over
each time the earth passes
through its fierce instars,
the tiny hammers and engines
of dropping leaves and wings
or shell casings, the crash of elk
and armies, clouds or continents.

Behind a curtain called rain
atoms overcast one another,
link and mate, each molecule
knits a new door. You know
how the world is. It spins.
It spins.

BROWN TENT

What she'll remember
is the moth.
Sitting there, Louise
forgets the day,
drinking Manhattans.
The woman opposite
stretches on the couch,
arranges herself
in the boneless
pose of the feline,
with the same
inverted V frown.
Louise despises her.
A small fire
in the birdbath
outside, a cardinal.
Benches like
baked loaves. Snow
is radioactive.
Don't eat it.
It never stops falling.
A kid in the corner
wraps himself
in a ballad.
His open guitar case
is salted with bills.

Through a tall window
lights begin to wash
the slopes. Skiers
carve S's in long chains,
braiding a private bliss
in gray and white.
Dusk slowly
erases the woman.
Beside Louise
a Luna moth is framed
on the wall. Its lime
hindwings curve
to slender yellow,
antenna red,
feathery as infant
ferns. Gorged on sumac,
persimmon and birch,
it once built a brown tent
for itself, then emerged
without a mouth.

REMOTE CONTROL

There are no rules
against fly hatch, the frenzied swarm
clouding eyes, ears. Who wants cruel
truths beneath the sea. Surface storms
are enough to break us. Dream
of cicada sound, a billion pewter
beads rinsing down a screen,
or of nights, rain muted.
I tell you, sometimes news splashes
into a room and empties your lungs.
Curl into whatever passes
for blue chicory. Practice a far-flung
frost. Protest, *that's not me, not my-*
knowing all the while that it's a lie.

JAKE'S ADVICE

You can take a line at dawn and find
the odd fish running like a blade
through butter, flaring like the sun.
There's always something. Take this cup here,
or a dish, say, cracked as an old face.
In the right light it can have the shine
of a girl. See, what I'm saying is
you gotta push through the sting. Always
some bit of shade. A bit of shade.

THE ORCHARD, SEPTEMBER 2001

Beneath a crushing
sky grapes perfume
the air

slump over
their supports.
The fruit farmer

sits on his tractor
idling.
His overalls

are made of oak.
Apple crates
balance in towers

between the rows.
Fallen apples soften
the ground.

In his palm,
a Macintosh.
Taste

its juicy sand,
that first bite
large in your throat.

A radio
feeds his ears,
skins the news.

The sun
unhinges
and falls down.

BOTH SIDES OF THE MOBIUS STRIP

The geometry of continents fitting
together is in proportion
to the dimensions of your voice
across three time zones,

and Pi goes as far as flashlight beams
into the ellipse of my own grandmother

making brown sugar sandwiches
on the Formica counter. The equilateral
triangle of winter-spring-fall frames
a solid center of summertime bicycles

cornering at angles so severe a string
from their handlebars must find its dotted

way to the center of the sun. What I mean is
your *hello* is a tangent from the Buster Brown
x-ray machine arrowing through
the square milk chute into our locked house.

ICE HOUSE

What do you owe,
moth whispers.

Some days the sky slams,
concrete sizzles.

Brother, I have no feet.

The air is iron
unbuttoning the moon.

ELEPHANTS NEVER FORGET

From eight miles out you can see across the Atlantic
to Margate's elephant, six-story survivor of rust and rot.
Born one of three siblings, to the brain of a New Jersey
financier, its body has outlasted them all. Photographs
fix the history, faint winking lights of a life span
much like a father's.

Threatened with a wrecking ball, the elephant
was moved inland and repaired, tin and paint
restored, despite heated protest and expense.
You can visit the elephant, lean from the howdah,
to stroke a shoulder, on certain days, at certain hours
rather like a nursing home.

You can climb the winding staircase of a rear leg
to the gastric pink interior, and then on to the
cavern behind the gray trunk, and red rimmed eyes.
A phrase or two is etched in the timbers. A swallow
flits in the rafters of the head like a lost thought
something like Alzheimer's.

There is a platform behind the window eyes.
From here you can see blank sky meet the horizon
of the Atlantic, watch storms gather and approach,
or simply stand with the elephant staring
out at the flat empty restless sea
just like a daughter.

BIOLUMINESCENCE

Swim alone in the dark.
 Dive to a pool lit by distant moons,
lanterns drowsing in the only ocean on earth,
their light dissolving to womb song.

 The spine wilts to muscle,
flaccid as mollusk, and lungs become sponges
filtering water into something pure,
the clean edge of sound outdistanced by sight.

Swim. Alone in the dark.

Dying people sometimes shine.

CANYON

When the day fries up all the birds
I could sit on this rock forevermore.
Guess we all remember being a child
watching some insect or other
creeping up a blade of grass.

In the canyon at night
there's a frog that screams
like a woman. Some folks
have a high and mighty
way of complicating every little thing.

Me, I believe in the river.
Whistle up a big copper moon
and you can witness God in that water.
The frog though, that sound
makes a person hope
the woman dies quick.

AN AWFUL STILLNESS

It's an awful stillness the moon feels
--William Stafford, "Looking Up At The Night"

The house turns to the moon.
Wait. It has always been like this,
    the yard as pale as fishbone.
I wake, listening. The dog nuzzles air
    in her dreams. Her body isn't meant
    to be reborn. Sweep back the covers.
Walk to that blind window where the house
    breathes. Listen to the blood racing
    and wonder what calls.
I have walked through currents
    on legs of stone. I know now
    there's a gate floating free. Touch here,
    this place where leaves knock.
You will survive this water.

DRAGONFLY AUGUST

One foot in the hum,
the other in sleep.

Surrender to the black, sister,
like water, noon heat
rising on turquoise, trembling.
Even cotton remembers

the field--a certain droning.
The fly-fat air is bursting.

THE CONSTANT HUM OF THE EARTH

A back screen door slams. Three dogs tangle-gallop
to his car, ears flaying dust and Imogene's slow smile
and question--"*Well, what do you know for sure?*"--
opens Boonville the way red tomatoes split clay soil,
taste of earth that blues the hydrangeas, covers coal

strip miners dig through generations.
At the Triangle, third shift dozes biscuits
through gravy and runny yolks, stirs coffee
with sausage fingers, talking
the last strike, the next strike, the big strike.

Labor Day red, white and by God blue flags
and Support Your Local signs stake every yard.
Back home for brain sandwiches and sweetened ice tea,
the dog-hot summer after dogwood spring.
And he knows again that hum running through

the planet two Japanese scientists discovered
sixteen octaves below middle C, like the whirring
cicada, or ceaseless draglines, black-bodied locusts
droning the horizon, and telephone wires passing
wrecks and births, the police scanner static

on kitchen tables, and neon lights at Dairy Treat
bluing teens like him before the hot thrum
of his 750 whined circles around the square
and fastened on, burying the toxin and itch deep
in the two-lane heading straight out of town.

JAKE, MOONLIGHTING

I was hanging on a wrench
then or blading a piece of road.
Those were hungry days,
my peacock time, leaning out
feeling the world, uncommonly stupid.

Knew a guy, a powder monkey
for the road outfit, could pick up
his old rifle and let down a deer
at a hundred yards, no scope,
standing off hand, no rest, no nothing.

He married a woman whose voice
could amputate the air. There's not
an apparatus of pulleys that could
get her to gaze up at the moon,
already bleached out and bowed.

THE EXCAVATOR

The murkiness of life
glows occasionally
in a pole barn
speared with whiskey light.

I cannot name all the rusted tools,
dismantled parts,
hanging on these walls
but can say: *gear, winch, blade, chain.*

The rind of the world called
since the cradle. He worked third shift at the mine,

days were for the cave
of his barn and old machines--
draglines, dozers, tractor guts.

A small window in a heated corner
is coated from the breath
of a thousand cigarettes,
ash thumbed, held in swollen fingers.

The air smells vaguely of oil,
wild onion, coal stripped from red clay, grass.

Men toss a loose word to each other,
cover eagerness
in solemn overalls, shuffling.

Remote as old newsprint,
an auctioneer begins to sell him off,
4 linear yards at a time.

STONES

If I stand alone
in his garage
among the big boots
and wire,
the compressed
talk of men,
their conversations
pass through my mind.
He liked hot mustard,
smelled of Old Spice.
    Men have a clean way
of dropping
a word or two
like stones
in the busy currents
of women.
    Somewhere
in the rafters
his voice comes back,
Well, that's all right,
    that's all right.

WORM MOON

March's full moon is called "Worm Moon"
--Old Farmer's Almanac

The moon is old tonight,
nicotine stained, sallow.
My father's in the moon,
fingered dull brass, worn
thin and pocked, a flat disk
slipping away one inch
and a half a year. He taught
the solar system with oranges
and the sun was a Florida
Red grapefruit, never said
Sputnik's dog was doomed
or that starshine beams
from space junk. The moon
is one weary socket in the
dead eye of night, though
yesterday, when he said
my name, that one word
stabbed the dust, a flag
to show we'd been.

NO WORD FOR GREEN

Smothered by vastness
a woman who looks

like a shot glass
says she hates horses,

the way they tear a
hole in memory.

Her roof simmers
under flat tires.

THE MAN AND THE BLUEFIN TUNA

He places the grocery sack next to him
in the car, escapes to the reds and yellows
deep into shades of black, squid ink
trees blowsy as anemones. Night creatures
swim by in the charcoal world. Neon
flashes *food/fuel* the way bamboo coral
fires blue rings in sequence. The man
and the bluefin tuna bend to the familiar scent
of the center-line and speed, speed, speed,
trance racing dark silhouettes, light garlands;
barreling past towns lit golden as roe. The man
accelerates. The flesh in the tin contracts.

HER FAVORITE STORY

And everyone was quiet
moving to the windows
from their desks and cupboards
or pianos to stand together, watching.

It was the last time
it snowed on earth.
March. I could tell you

all the facts, the finite dimensions
of depth, duration, degrees

but we reached for it falling.
And it fell so slowly, softly
bandaging edges,
each flake particular.

And for a time
we were monkeys
and monks, kicking
through the drifts
or solemn as candles.

It is hard to tell you
of snow. It was
like the ash, but colder.

COLD

In the wake of a current
a star falls. It is the stuff of story.
Who can tell what we hope for?
    Once I knew a song.
It lies in my mind green as parsley.
Do you remember it?
Sit beside me so we might appear
anything but frozen
an eyelash away from zero.

PROBABILITIES

And it's true
you can read bootprints
like the palm of someone's hand
knowing he works in Oregon, say,
drinks Coors and prays
his wife, who sings in the choir,
won't disturb the covers
or the perfectly arranged pillows
to find him gone, just *gone*
some day, like those broken men
out on the pier relying on
the pure chance of a fish
hitting their lines, saving them
just one more day.

JAKE, DYING

My born-again sister clucked
about hatching new. This dark

rises like a fevered river
and I don't know yet
what salt air smells like,

      never felt a flash of canvas
above my head on an ocean.

Lead me to the reason we carry rifles
and I'll put all my bullets on the table.
There's wings inside an egg, she said.

Maybe that's enough.
   Knowing about the wings.

THE SHAPE OF FEAR

Millipede knows. Tuck and roll
before seeping cyanide. A chuckwalla
balloons his body to wedge
a sandstone crevice. In black-knotted
forests, when a bear's breathing peels the spine,
fold to the fetal, huddle small, bald
as a huckleberry or the bundle a spider
makes to save her dinner live.

In the gullet of the sea, mindless as rain
before the tuna attack, sardines spin
into a bait ball; a thousand thousand tails snap
and turn, racing the silver strings of their bodies
into a whorl of matter, not liquid, not solid.
From beneath, tuna, dolphins crash
the mercury mass.

Shearwaters plunge from above,
swim-flying to the center
until the reeling sphere unravels in the dark.
Make no mistake, fear is eyeball round.

GRASSES

    It's still the same, Joanna,
the way the ocean works,
in the manner of myth, imperfect as prayer.

Something visits my brain, rests there
nosing the straw.

Why don't we watch against
the way stars fail us in winter,
or the odd custom of frost ferning glass?

Twilight wicks away and night extends.
Never mind the stars. They're drifting further out.

What matters, I think, is the marrow of grasses.
There are so many lives to know. They are not
swallowed, only released.

Apprentice yourself to a fool and the small beast
inside your brain rises on stilts.

About the Author

Marion Boyer received her B.A. from Purdue University and taught English in Indiana before moving to Kalamazoo, Michigan where she has lived with her husband since 1973. While raising their two sons she attended graduate school at Western Michigan University receiving a Master's degree in Communication. In 1992, Marion joined the faculty of Kalamazoo Valley Community College as a full-time instructor where she teaches courses in public speaking, interpersonal communication, intercultural communication and oral interpretation.

She has published essays and poems in diverse publications. Her essays, frequently written about her travel experiences, have appeared in magazines such as <u>Canoe & Kayak</u>, <u>Paddler Magazine</u> and <u>American Whitewater</u>. <u>Educational Travel Review</u> selected a collection of her work as "best of issue," awarding her a trip for two to London, England. Her writing also appears in the anthology <u>Voices of Michigan.</u>

Marion's poetry has been published in numerous literary journals such as *The Spoon River Poetry Review, Midwest Quarterly, The Atlanta Review, Driftwood Review, Crab Creek Review, The MacGuffin, Midnight Mind,* and *Rhino,* among others.